Dear Parent

Your child's love of pictures encourages his love of learning.

There are many similar words in English and German. Did you know there are many words with the same spelling and meaning in English and German? As you learn the English words, you will automatically know the German equivalent as well. Going through the alphabet many such words, mainly nouns, were highlighted and age appropriately selected and illustrated. In this way children are introduced to vocabulary in both languages simultaneously. The vivid, colourful and dynamic illustrations relate to the child's reality.

The magical ABC is aimed at children of ages 3 to 7 years old.

- **3-4 year old's** are able to find, point to and learn the words illustrated with the assistance of a parent or teacher.
- **5-6 year old's** are beginning to recognize letters and associate them with their sound. In so doing they will be able to relate the letter to the word.
- For **6-7 year old's** reading and recognizing the words and appreciating the pictures for themselves will be an enjoyable experience.

The book uses pictures of familiar items easily recognized by children and captures their attention.

The large uppercase and lowercase letter appears on the page along with the words, in both English and German. The list of words on each page are in random order. The same letter in the illustrations is large and clearly shows the items the letter portrays.

The magical ABC book has a predictable pattern in the way the objects are presented to the reader. First the letter in both cases, then the words, in both English and German, followed by the illustrations of all the words, on the opposite/following page.

This English German Bilingual book is perfect for children in an environment where they are exposed to both languages throughout the day.

Many words both in English and German:

- **sound the same,** such as: baby, computer, gold.
- **sound the same, but are written differently.** For example, mouse - Maus, bear - Bär, fish - Fisch.
- **Are written the same, but are pronounced differently.** For example, name, astronaut, bus, orange, ball, pilot, tiger.
- **Slightly different in writing and pronunciation,** such as: music – musik, mask – Maske, noodle – Nudel, telescope – Teleskop.

The table below shows changes which occur between the two languages.

In English a...	becomes a …. in German	Examples
p	pf, ff and f	apple-Apfel, pan-Pfanne, plant-Pflanze,
t	z, tz, s and ss	water-Wasser, salt-Salz
k	ch and ck	milk-Milch, book-Buch, cook-Koch
k, c or ch	k	card-Karte, cheese-Käse
ch, sh, s	sch	fish-Fisch, snow-Schnee
c	z	circus-Zirkus, dance-Tanz
th	d, t	bath-Bad, weather-Wetter
d	t	garden-garten, bed-Bett
b f, or v	b	calf-Kalb, seven-Sieben
to -(l)y, -al, -ic or -	-ig, -lich, -isch and -ität	electricity-Elektrizität, underground-unterirdisch

THE
Magical
DAS
Magische

My first English-German bilingual book
Mein erstes Englisch-Deutsch bilinguales Buch

Thalia Evangelidis
Illustrated by Wesley Paixão

For
Sotiri,

Thank you to Wesley for the illustrations,
Dot, Michail and Nathalie for their assistance

Aa Bb Cc Dd Ee

Ff Gg Hh Ii Jj Kk

Ll Mm Nn Oo Pp

Qq Rr Ss Tt Uu

Vv Ww Xx Yy Zz

apple	Apfel
apricot	Aprikose
anchor	Anker
ant	Ameisen
astronaut	Astronaut
axe	Axt
alarm	Alarm

Bb

bed	Bett
bear	Bär
ball	Ball
balloon	Ballon
bus	Bus
bath	Badewanne
brush	Bürste
boat	Boot
baby	Baby
banana	Banane
bee	Biene
bread	Brot
broom	Besen
bush	Bush
butter	Butter

Bb

café	Café
clown	Clown
cowboy	Cowboy
computer	Computer
cent	Cent
choir	Chor
club	Club

dolphin	Delfin
dinosaur	Dinosaurier
diamond	Diamant
dragon	Drachen
detective	Detektiv
doctor	Doktor
disk	Diskette

Dd

earth	Erde
elephant	Elefant
egg	Ei
England	England
explosion	Explosion
echo	Echo
electricity	Elektrizität

fire	Feuer
flame	Flamme
fireman	Feuerwehrmann
fox	Fuchs
fish	Fisch
frog	Frosch
feather	Feder
field	Feld
flag	Flagge
film	Film
footprint	Fußabdruck

gorilla	Gorilla
ghost	Geist
giraffe	Giraffe
goose	Gans
grasshopper	Grashüpfer
grass	Gras
gift	Geschenk
gold	Gold
glass	Glas

house	Haus
helicopter	Hubschrauber
hen	Henne
hamburger	Hamburger
hat	Hut
hay	Heu
honey	Honig
hammer	Hammer
handbag	Handtasche
hand	Hand
helmet	Helm
hill	Hügel
hundred	Hundert

Hh

igloo	Iglo
insect	Insekt
island	Insel
instrument	Instrument
internet	Internet
Italy	Italien

jacket	Jacke
jeans	Jeans
jewel	Juwel
juggler	Jongleur
jet	Jet

king	König
kingdom	Königreich
kitchen	Küche
kitten	Kätzchen
kangaroo	Känguru
kettle	Kessel
kiss	Kuss

lion	Löwe
leopard	Leopard
lamb	Lamm
lighthouse	Leuchtturm
light	Licht
ladder	Leiter
land	Land
lamp	Lampe
landscape	Landschaft

mother	Mutter
mom	Mama
man	Mann
mask	Maske
motorbike	Motorrad
market	Markt
mosquito	Moskito
milk	Milch
mouse	Maus
medal	Medaille
moon	Mond
metal	Metall
microphone	Mikrofon
mill	Mühle
mine	Mine
music	Musik

Mm

nose	Nase
nut	Nuss
nail	Nagel
needle	Nadel
nest	Nest
neighbour	Nachbar
neighbourhood	Nachbarschaft
night	Nacht
number	Nummer
net	Netz
noodle	Nudel

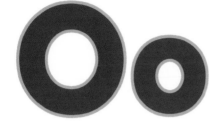

ocean	Ozean
omelett	Omelett
orange	Orange
olive oil	Olivenöl
olive	Olive
oven	Ofen
officer	Offizier
ox	Ochse
orca	Orca

pirate	Pirat
palm	Palme
parrot	Papagei
pirate ship	Piratenschiff
princess	Prinzessin
pilot	Pilot
popcorn	Popcorn
pyramid	Pyramide
parcel	Paket

Pp

quartet	Quartett
quartz	Quarz
qualification	Qualifikation
quark	Quark
quince	Quitte

rainbow	Regenbogen
rocket	Rakete
rose	Rose
radio	Radio
rat	Ratte
rain	Regen
ruby	Rubin
ring	Ring
red	Rot
robber	Räuber

sailboat	Segelboot
sail	Segel
starfish	Seestern
sand	Sand
sun	Sonne
sock	Socke
skeleton	Skelett
ship	Schiff
shoe	Schuhe
swan	Schwan
snake	Schlange
shadow	Schatten
snail	Schnecke
star	Stern
spider	Spinne

Ss

tower	Turm
tiger	Tiger
telephone	Telefon
toaster	Toaster
toast	Toast
tea	Tee
teapot	Teekanne
table	Tisch
tablecloth	Tischdecke
tunnel	Tunnel
telescope	Teleskop

universe	Universum
Underground	U-Bahn
underground	unterirdisch
underwater world	Unterwasserwelt
underwear	Unterwäsche
uniform	Uniform
Uranus	Uranus

video	Video
vase	Vase
volcano	Vulkan
volleyball	Volleyball
vitamin	Vitamin

Ww

water	Wasser
wave	Welle
whale	Wal
wolf	Wolf
wind	Wind
weather	Wetter
wool	Wolle
worm	Wurm
waterfall	Wasserfall
wine	Wein
watchman	Wächter
white	Weiß
walrus	Walross

Ww

 xylophone   Xylophon

 yacht   Yacht

Zz

zoo	Zoo
zebra	Zebra
zigzag	Zickzack
Zeppelin	Zeppelin
zucchini	Zucchini
zebu	Zebu

THE ALPHABET - DAS ALPHABET

Aa		**Bb** 		**Cc**	
Dd		**Ee**		**Ff**	
Gg		**Hh**		**Ii**	
Jj		**Kk**		**Ll**	
Mm		**Nn**		**Oo**	
Pp		**Qq**		**Rr**	
Ss		**Tt**		**Uu** 	
Vv		**Ww**		**Xx** 	
Yy		**Zz**			

THE END - DAS ENDE